PR

NA'.

"vermette portrays a wide array of strong, complicated, absolutely believable women, and through them and their hardships offers readers sharp views of race and class issues. This is slice-of-life storytelling at its finest."

—*Publishers Weekly*, starred review

"It's unsurprising that a novel by a poet would be beautifully written ... *The Break* is an astonishing act of empathy, and its conclusion is heartbreaking."

—*The Globe and Mail*

"In *The Break*, the characters may be Métis, but the motivations and emotions are surely universal. This is an accomplished writer who will go far."

—Margaret Atwood

PRAISE FOR *RIVER WOMAN*

"Intensely political and personal ... A beautiful and resonant book."
—*Prairie Fire*

"In *river woman*, katherena vermette marshals the maternal energy of the river to spin the lyric poem into something that is awash with vitality. This ethic of care, which each section bears and ricochets about, has at its core a project of repair or nourishment, not just of the natural, but of those of us entangled with it. This us, vermette deftly shows, is not an empty thing, but is instead teeming with Indigenous life—'we are the earth you are hurting.' We are the river and, in this, we are without end, regardless of what history swells in us. Pick up this book and listen for the musicality of our beautiful rebellion!"
—Billy-Ray Belcourt, author of *This Wound Is a World*,
winner of the 2018 Griffin Poetry Prize

"'A snake carved / into prairie grass,' *river woman* is a collection that will stay with you, question you, live in you. One cannot simply tread the surface of its open invitation. There are many layers here below the poetic surface, and vermette is singer-guide to the true depths of this river. It's a work to be read, shared, and read again."
—Liz Howard, author of *Infinite Citizen of the Shaking Tent*,
winner of the 2016 Griffin Poetry Prize

procession

procession

procession

katherena vermette

ANANSI

House of Anansi Press is committed to protecting our natural environment. This
book is made of material from well-managed FSC®-certified forests, recycled
materials, and other controlled sources.

House of Anansi Press is a Global Certified Accessible™ (GCA by Benetech)
publisher. The ebook version of this book meets stringent accessibility standards
and is available to readers with print disabilities.

29 28 27 26 25   1 2 3 4 5

Library and Archives Canada Cataloguing in Publication

Title: Procession : Katherena Vermette.
Names: Vermette, Katherena, 1977- author.
Identifiers: Canadiana (print) 20250162121 | Canadiana (ebook) 20250169657 |
ISBN 9781487013523 (softcover) | ISBN 9781487013530 (EPUB)
Subjects: LCGFT: Poetry.
Classification: LCC PS8643.E74 P76 2025 | DDC C811/.6—dc23

Cover design: Alysia Shewchuk
Cover artwork: *Universe* by Tracy Charette Fehr, 2024
Interior design: Laura Brady
Typesetting: Lucia Kim

*House of Anansi Press is grateful for the privilege to work on and create from the
Traditional Territory of many Nations, including the Anishinabeg, the Wendat, and the
Haudenosaunee, as well as the Treaty Lands of the Mississaugas of the Credit.*

With the participation of the Government of Canada
Avec la participation du gouvernement du Canada | Canadä

*We acknowledge for their financial support of our publishing program the Canada
Council for the Arts, the Ontario Arts Council, and the Government of Canada.*

Printed and bound in Canada

for those who came before
and those who come after

"Beauty is truth, truth beauty,—that is all
Ye know on earth, and all ye need to know."

—*John Keats*

contents

contents

grimoire

before you were this
you were
the dream
of a hundred martyrs
you were
a wish
the sort that lingers
under young girl whispers
into young girl ears

a spark in a loving eye
prayer floating in wind

you were as light
as the seeds
sprinkled about
this wide red earth

now you are
a ridge
brief plateau
on the mountain of revolution
one the ancestors
looked up to
and said
one day

your birth has taken
centuries
a labour that nearly killed

them all
you are
now

and you have
so much magick in you
stories that have waited
lifetimes
to be told

Biindigen

Aaniin

the spirit in me
sees the spirit in you

like namaste
this word first acknowledges
the brightness
that comes
from inside
goes out

before
anything else
my spirit
light
greets yours

what better way is there
to begin

*Anishinaabemowin greeting—direct translation, something
like, my spirit greets your spirit

Taanishi Kiiya

not only do I greet you
but I ask how
you are

how you feel
or how you have
come to be

here or maybe what
brought us
all here
what could
make us all
so lucky
to be

I am so glad
to see you
to say these words to you
know them
know you

*Michif greeting, direct translation something like, hello, how
are you?

Biindigen

come in
take up the space
I have made for you

wherever I am
there will always be
a home for you

more surprise
than expectation
but there is a place
here for you
to be
as much
as you are

I have made myself
as open
as possible
to let you be
come

*Anishinaabemowin—welcome

Nimaamaa Aki / La Tayr Maamaa

pregnancy has never been
easy for me
my skin softens
swells
limbs become tangents
to womb
I am uneasy
without even a dubious
sense of control

I am not
like her
she creates constantly
gestates
births
feeds
watches it all grow
only to watch much of it die

then she chills
rests
does it all over again

nothing about her is extraneous
everything in her is creation
she can be gentle
and strong

even as we walk all over her
her heart remains full
pace never rushed
or slowed
she just rolls
onward

*Mother Earth

Nookomis Giizis / La Leun Noohkoom

old
grey
grated with age
like cheese

she watches over
and lights up
for us
reflects but
sings her own song
quiet
constant
solid as our earth mother
she gave that to her
and she makes
waves

we can feel her
know she's close
even when
everything is dark

but we're wrong
she isn't the one who changes
we are the ones
who keep moving
away from her

*Grandmother Moon

Anishinaabemowin

this is what came before the world

it was this
that called it
into being

so much older than these
words we speak now
it has flowed through
more of your ancestors
than any other
it has flowed within me
even when I don't
understand

especially then

*the language

Michif

grown of parts
older than the whole
twined together like braid
worn but new

made for trade
made to transcend otherness
made
a part

to be understood
by as many people as possible

not half but both
not both but own

*the language

procession

you are only here
to honour your ancestors
and prepare for your children

more inclusive version:

you are only here
                    to learn from those who came before
and make space
                    for those who come after

those who came before/ancestors

those who come after/children

you are
            at once

burdened by responsibility
                            made free of it

what they did
        what they will do
                all we do

maybe responsibility is
the wrong word

    perhaps
        honour
                learn
   prepare
       make
       space
          before
             after

you inherit
    and you
            pass on

only going
     for
       ward

         n

      o

it's the Earth that   moves

and only in a circle

                    sun

                              moon
               time
                                        stay in
                         place

maybe moving is the wrong word

you
only
are

          at once
                    belong
                              and are

                              belonged to

grounded

                                   and spirit

what you were before/children

what you will be after/ancestors

                                you are
                            at once
        only

   and
   all

carry memory

photographs

if they were only
thoughts they would
exist solely in our minds
so they are not only
thoughts

if they were only
bodies they would go
with death if they were only
feeling they would fade
in a changed mood
only spirit
they would lift
in the wind
fly off and away if
they were only photographs
those faces no
thicker than
paper flat
faded

if they were only
that they wouldn't
so clearly
look back

if it were a river

the road moves in
and out of the bush
weaves bends
dissects jackpine
cedar
ever grey around stone
the road
mimics natural curves
as if it were carved by them
as if it were a river

but there's nothing
organic
about the road
trees were cut down
stumps pulled out
earth blasted
open
death cleared the bush
death and tired brown men
who worked for long hours
short pay
their lives impoverished
by everything but air
space
bush
there was always too much
bush

my grandfather did that
led a team of horses
four-wide
to clear the trees
pick through rock
smooth earth
until flat
he lived in a camp
all summer
tall canvas tent
cot
campfire and cigarettes
every night
short friendships
with long stories

he'd return near
first snowfall
his back still dark
from the sun
bent a little more
each year
dirt in the creases
of skin that never
quite washed all the way
away

winter life was a different season
noise of children
a wife who made faces
in every photo

stove always alight
bills always paid
black tea and cigarettes
every evening

you wonder which
he loved more
which place he lay
longing for the other
or if he spent his life
balanced
between the two

the road folds
around each turn
asphalt softened
by snow
rain worn
edges bend
through birch
poplar
nearly natural curves
as if it were the river
that was trying to be
the road

consider

light
eyes
subject
focus
flash
range

focal length
motion
depth
mode
balance
particularly

white balance
exposure

grin

twinkle-eyed and cocksure
Uncle was a man
who had the world by the balls
who looked into the camera
like a cat that ate something
canary or cream

he did have it all
beautiful wife and kids
job at the trains
kind you could retire from
house big enough
to fit even that head

he knew his way
around a pool table
straight to a lady's heart
with a wink
smirked moustache
he had them all
he was so
cock-eyed
almost certain

parts

aperture
lens
shutter
release

path of light
view finder
image sensor
prism
film

diaphragm
memory

your ancestors there

you can see
your children
in you

reflection of a now-
long-gone face that smiles
from behind
the camera

you can see
your ancestors there
all your relations in
all of you

her story, notes

carry memory
photos frame identity
learn how to read them
visual literacy
photography is a social practice
literal self-preservation
negative / space
narrative / creation

family photo albums tended to be
tended by the Matriarchs
created by

established her identity
curated own narrative
highly edited
controlled
sometimes the only control
how she understood
her experience in the world

how else would she have spoken
to you
to anyone
about her life
her family

made her own story
not her own

Mamère

you never talked about your secrets
the bad things you held
superstitiously close
as if giving voice
would only
let them out

lost your mom so young
moved to the city for school
didn't finish
married too young

baby boys all in a row
twin boys who died at birth
we don't even know their names
only that you refused
to return to the hospital
the following year
our next Uncle was born at home

in the flood of 1950
when the river pushed too close
you left that house
never to go back
never to live so close
or trust
the water
again

you lost
husband and son
the same year

how is this you?
these sad
empty facts
but

you're kneaded dough
made too quick and lumpy
you're burnt raisin pie
so good it's still raved about

you're the *coronation street*
omnibus every Sunday morning
all the characters you knew
better than your own cousins
and talked back to
yelled at
cried with

you're detailed lessons
how to roll cigarettes just so
not too tight
but I always did
and you only smiled
smoothed the stuffed tube
between your fingers
sprinkled out the extra tobacco
carefully piled
the medicine and swept

it back into the pouch
you're absolutely nothing ever wasted

you're noxzema on a nightstand
stale scotch mints
on the table by the door
in a fancy glass bowl
with the lid always on

you are long
sleepy jokes
that made no real sense
but made you laugh too hard
before you even got to the punch line
you are full belly laughs
the kind that get into everything

even bad things
never let out

endings only begin

soft with age
and touch
photographs in piles
unorganized

faces echo familiarity
names lost

Ithinkthatwasthatcouldhavebeenlookslikeyou
likehercouldberight?maybeprettysure

we search at the edges
a dream gone at waking

just there
still there

so many so old unsmiling
backs straight
performing stoicism
feet planted on land
recategorized
but earth like them
unchanged

every album is always
incomplete
every frame cuts
something off
endings only begin
something else

and all these bodies
still alive
in your body

your body is a sovereign nation

first land of belonging
last circle of kinship
homeland
homeplace
all you are made of
all you have to give

sacred space of spirit
light
as under siege as mother
earth
like her you can be destroyed
like her you are not
yet and nothing
anyone can ever do
will negate your sacredness
the purity of your spirit
no matter how scarred
you are
divine

your body is sovereign—
a place no one can tell you
no
here you are more than chief and council
president or prime minister
here you sit
in assembly with your ancestors
and descendants
convene in lodge

come to consensus
no one else is
consulted

my body is a nation
lucky to live in my home territory
wherever else i go
i am a visitor
and will act accordingly
but wherever else i go
i am here
so still
home

make beautiful

southdale 1979

cold wind over
empty fields
an adolescent part of town
awkward
not fully formed

iced air puffed out like
daddy's cigarette smoke
feet tucked under
this so small body
legs hug new curb

once you were a turtle
skin shelled
playing with the smallest
stones

mom always thought you were
the saddest kid in the world
playing all alone like that

but you knew
sand tells stories
you have to be quiet to
hear

surrey 1980

walking home up the long
mountain road—
a wave of grey smoke overlapped the clouds
the whole ground rumbled
(you can still feel this
in your chest
all these years later)

dad picked you up
ran faster than you could ever
go
yelled over your head
at mom and brother

locked the doors behind you
he leaned into the prickly blue screen
told you to stay away from the windows
the soviets he said
or maybe the east germans

you don't say a word
waiting for the next rumble
or worse
mom made soup in the kitchen
brother watched
the newscaster's white hair bounced
beside a picture of an innocent looking
mountain

saint helen so close
down in washington state
a lazy old volcano woke up a bit
stretched out her abundant bulk
and belched
dad turned off the tv
mom ladled chicken noodle into bowls

you made your barbies heroes
victorious against
tyrannical g.i. joe oppressors

there at the start of something that never was
you played war

berkshire bay 1981

dad drove the red vw van
right up to front door
you moved in
without touching grass

trains coughed
giggled as they passed
so close you thought they would
rub up against the house

summer dried out
the long bush of tired saplings
along the tracks
another unfinished
neighbourhood

you risked the climb to see
a nest abandoned
egg shells delicate
periwinkle
brother put one on his finger
held it up to the sun

you were so scared
(you were always so scared)
held on to the swaying branch
took another shell in your palm
studied the taupey insides
looked for any sign of
the guts it once grew

real mother 1982

your mother is white
like she won the white lottery
white with her blond hair
blue eyes—
a conventional beauty

she is your biological mother
though your whole life people
always thought you and your brother
were adopted
would assume
with furrowed brows
tilted heads
those poor brown-ish children
they would mutter
how good you are
they'd tell her
and she'd laugh
say no really they
came from me

if it is as they say
our mothers are
our first mirrors
first face we learn
the one we take a while to separate from
hers was yours—
your white gold-medal-winning
reflection

she used to love to tell you the story
of when you first came back from bc
you were three
started being rebellious
and creepy
(it's worth noting you continued to be
a rebellious and creepy child long after this)

you would tell her you were
going back
to the mountains
back to your real mother

would call
your real mother
could barely reach phone
only grab the receiver
put it to ear
and scratch circles on wall
far below the rotary
tiny fingernails cut paint
while you whispered into the dial tone
glaring at your actual mother as you did

she would tell this story to everyone
sitting at the kitchen table
over that same phone she could actually reach
she'd tell it with a laugh
like you were just another cute kid
but you knew it freaked her out
and you knew that was why
you kept doing it

you don't remember what you said
to your real mother
what you said so quiet
but you remember her—
a lady with long dark hair
plaid shirt
backdrop of mountains
and wooden carvings—
a truck stop likely

some stranger with whom you felt kinship
someone who
looked like you

Snake 1984

slam of cheap-wood back door
padlocks unravelled
bikes freed

the day hot already
you race behind him
silently begging to catch up
but he liked to go fast

over shortcuts pavements
grass crisscross bays
he'd gather
compatriots
other messy half-brown
kids in this almost-suburb

off into the bush you'd follow
a dozen kids on—whatever they had—
foot bike handlebars
into the yet-to-be-developed wild
the glorious in-between

you were always last
through dreary clearings
old furniture empty bottles
long cigarette butts as prized
as jewels
artefacts of night

beyond to the gravel pits
beside the train yard
sand mountains slashed with
tire tracks '

looked over by the ghosts
in the old abandoned meat-packing building
on the other side
four long storeys of brick
broken windows dark

but here you were safe
with Snake
all your compatriots
who'd race
the day away

you watched on
your banana-seat bike far too
back-heavy to catch any real air
but Snake's bmx could really compete

long chain across
his jean vest frayed
at the shoulders like joey jeremiah

flew up the slopes that passed
for high in this flat place

took bets
won half-smokes

coins for sev
he was nine

no one would leave
until the sun started
going down
the old meat-packing building's
shadows got too long
crept toward you

we raced back through
bush without looking
around

sand dusty
slurpees
penny candy

that awkward balance of cold cup
on handle bars

home to hot dogs
tomato soup
long silences
forced baths

tv from a couch that was
as brown as your
summer-soaked skin

waiting for morning
Snake's voice through the vent
between your rooms

get up
he'd wake you
let's go
and you would

winakwa road 1985

blizzard hit
two months after your parents separated
brother visiting
bored already

mother rented a beta machine
bickered about ungratefulness

then they got sick —
high fevers
worse moods

you were sent through snow
down back lane
past medical centre
over parking lot
to the video store
you wanted to go
(badly)

your long blue coat with
unmatching black ski pants
mother wrapped you tight in her own scarf
walked you to the building's back door
sent off with kiss
and laugh

you hobbled into quiet white
fresh cold

mountains to climb
new paths to carve
an untouched sea all yours

at store you had money enough
for three movies
so picked:
Educating Rita (mom's favourite)
Ewoks (your favourite)
and took a long time to choose
perfect chuck norris movie for brother
(he had many favourites
and you don't remember which one)

on the way back
paths made were gone
so you made new ones

mother waited where you left her
pink velour bathrobe leaning
hot forehead onto cold glass
brother asleep on steps behind

then you got to
huddle on couch with blankets
their extra heat warming
your frostbite
you watched every movie
ate all the popcorn

until you saw a lone figure
out the big window
someone trudging slow down
the empty white street

dad came in
with wind and fogged glasses
cold embedded in his rough skin

missed you all
he told you
walked the whole way

you are the sky 1987

no friends in this new place
old houses
huge elms
kids that looked like you
even a new brother

mom likely tired of having to
entertain you
gave you extra hilroy notebooks
pink ones
extras
ones none of you wanted
here write she said
you're good at writing

you remember thinking
am I?
you held on to that compliment
for years
(still do)

you wrote a poem
only because it was
less daunting
than a whole story

it went:

When I look up at the sky
When I look higher than high

I see your face
Looking down at mine
You are the sky which makes me dream
Dream of happy things
Or of horrors and screams
But if I hear the horrors and screams
I am comforted to know
You're looking down at me

a version of god you'd been taught
tried on for size
love fraught with fear
misuse but
promised soothing
(tracks)

worldly 1989

if god was so loving why
would he care about worship?

why did we have to thank him
for the good
but not admonish him for the bad?

you think you've added language
you didn't have back then
but you were a pretty weird
precocious little thing
so who knows

your full notebooked (not pink)
questions were as follows:
1. if we were all god's children why
    was only one of us worshipped?
    why is jesus so special? (in hindsight
    this one is pretty basic considering
    your attention-getting siblings)
2. if god really wanted to make the world better
    why didn't he make his one worshipped child
    a brown kid—or better, a brown girl! so the world
    would treat them better (twelve-year-old you had no real
    understanding of how jesus was actually a brown man
    made white)

another thought about how most churches were too
institutional
against what xianity truly was

but
pretty sure that came from the
mennonite revulsion to all things too
"worldly"

(worldly – a definition – too materialistic
full of meaninglessness and void of godliness
examples include: rituals, possessions, intellectualism,
vain people who are at best silly and at worst satanic)

at twelve you were hella smart
abstract thinking hit you hard
at some point you concluded
you were not a xian
big epiphany for you
announcement
a coming-out of sorts:

your mom thought you were just being
rebellious and creepy
as she did
your stepfather likely laughed
as was his way
your brothers probably said nothing
and/or threw pillows at you
as was theirs
you were treated as a wayward child who only
needed time to see the light
(you know this for sure because this
is how you were always treated)

your friends took it seriously though:
one so worried about yours
and hers and everyone's souls
took you to her aunt's revival meeting
where you watched her succumb to
speaking in tongues
something you had always known as super
worldly
you were scared and wanted to leave
but they had pop and chips for afters
and not even no-name kind
so you stayed
open-mouthed moaned a bit so you
would look the part

another gave you a book called
Religions of the World
told you she was there to talk
when you were done
the book had a chapter on each:
judaism
hinduism
buddhism
one for each of the many xian denominations
shockingly they all seemed somehow incomplete
had something wrong with them

the last and longest chapter started with:
those believers known far and wide
for their unmatched devotion and dedication ...
and then you knew it was bullshit
no one thought of jehovah's witnesses that way

religion-less you stumbled
into adolescence
loved Ceremony
the one good thing your stepfather
ever showed you
wandered around belief systems
wondering which could be yours
came to think
things closest to nature
purest of the earth
seem truest

whatever god there was lived in everything
untouched by dreaded worldliness
yet full of the real one

you didn't even have to do anything
but look around
at the sky maybe
like your old poem
but with less gaslighting

make beautiful 1992

written in pencil erased
erased erased until the paper was soft
almost see-through

poem rhymed:
shed a tear for days passed by
for all the times now gone
shed a tear for all the memories
that the sun had shone

you cringe now
didn't then
didn't even notice

was half-assed sheepish
as it was read aloud
at a funeral

but the worst was
after when relatives put
hands hesitantly
to your shoulder
said that was nice

what you wrote
was nice

you didn't want to hear it
be reminded
likely blushed

also knew it didn't matter
poem had already done its job

it held your grief
took it out of you
made it beautiful
cringey but
beautiful

didn't read yourself until years later
poems kept journal-hidden
writing was for holed-off
spaces filled with only

scribbling
lapses in brilliance

reading your most intimate thoughts out loud
in front of people
real live ones?!

Marvin Francis said
you're a writer if you're writing
it's in the doing

you don't believe in good
no one is good
and everybody can be
good is completely subjective

you know this because
for many many
many long years good was only
one kind of person
colonized as everything else
good doesn't matter

writing is one of two things—
it's for you
or it's for other people

if it's just for you it's pure action
activity
words to page
done

breathe
feel better

if it's for other people
there is just another long
long step of making thoughts
legible

but that's it
that's writing
the rest is just business

we don't do art to be good
we get good by doing art
but real good art is the love of it

you got to love it
if you don't like this
pen to paper
fingertips to keys
then you have to find something else to do
then you really are not-good from the out-set

if you love it then
the rest is only drudgery

you forget this
get distracted
with all the always
somethings and everything elses

but you knew
as a mourning fifteen-year-old
with helpless rhymes
and no real love for herself but
she knew how to put her pain
into action
to make it beautiful

and she really
really knew
the rest of it
didn't matter

behold the Matriarchs

gather gather
roar and rabble

cast the Circle
and behold the Matriarchs

wee ones growing
in covens and classrooms

old ones honoured
in lodges and love

hardworking ones hustling
in corporations and co-ops

we are all making magick

from the kitchen witches
brewing care on stoves

to the artist witches
binding spells in paint and pages

boss bitch witches
taking names on the top floor

this is what a Matriarch looks like

we all come from Matriarchs
some of us lucky to be so close

to know
our Teachings from our living Elders

song to drum to
heartbeat

others have to reach back
centuries or only
know it in bones

knowledge passed from Matriarch
to newly born Matriarch

still in moving blood
yet we all somehow know

what Medicines to pick for healing
how to twist a babe in womb

how to whisper stories
to keep one
another
safe

we know

that this world has never worked as either/or
only as both and all and every

we know

our true selves are based on Spirit
not body parts

we know
we are all water carriers

this is what revolution looks like:

one small person
making more from little

one tiny movement
weaving hope into bleak

and seeing thru and to
the other side

witches be bitchin

Matriarchy recognizes
we all have a place and space

Ancestor to newly born
Ancestor

this was always
the way

(so mote it be
so blessed fucking be)

Matriarchy/dreamtime

not even

1

stories you tell
words you assign
are not experience
no matter how hard
you try

don't name
don't describe
feel
own
living is its own art
without words
without you
and with you

it's you
and not
even

2

I am feeling
my age growing
out my grey lines
map my living
I stare at
the routes I've taken
every day my skin wears
where I've been

3

this professor once told me
why he only dated
his students—
said after staring at young faces
all day
he didn't want to go home and look
at one as old as his
told me with a laugh
like it was funny

4

live life
as if
you've chosen it
you are your own
sun this world
your creation
spellcraft
every day

5

what if
we are living all our lives
at once
every choice
not taken
is still going
inside our lines
and pathways
neuro
skin
otherwise

every one still
everyone
you
and not
even

girl at café in rain at sunset smoking cigarette with long marble holder writing poetry

I love the french. the unironic way their poets talk about
sorrow, love, despair, desire, their precious precious hearts

my heart is broken. long live my heart

Michif affinity to french
more taught than felt
yet there is
something in the kohl eyes, spontaneous bangs,
languid, sexy depressions, I'm so
french sometimes

stop trying to make french happen

Mamère loved all things french, english, went to montreal
whenever she could, her sister lived there. they sat on the stoops
of ste catherine's, whispered truth (gossiped), despaired over
their love (husbands), waved off children and cigarette smoke
(no holders), undoubtedly she corrected her accent when
she went there (they make fun of it).
she coded before coding was cool

the Elder has passed. long live the Elder

I want to live on the other side of this wreckage, want to
sip things, look fulfilled, I want to nap gloriously on a chaise
lounge in the sun with a book slipping from my fingers to floor.
I want to appropriately mourn torrid affairs only to gracefully
stumble to the next

prop my feet on a woven bistro chair while old men tell me
stories all afternoon, not noticing how I gaze into middle distance
and say nothing, if interrupted I will comment on brilliant architecture
but really I am thinking of a boy who made me unmade

oh wait I do do that
you said do do

I want to walk in rain all night, face turned up to where the stars are,
 just behind those clouds, I can feel them

french is dead. long live Michif

things you can say about me when I am dead:

really did stick her feet into a lot of oceans
(no euphemism)

had a lot of kids (four)
loved them fiercely
mama-bear-like

had magick and magic
really did
was blessed
knew it

made up stories in her head
some amused her
some healed things
wrote them down
others read them
she hopes they were maybe
amused
healed

really sucked at being a good wife
secretly (not so secretly) wanted
a good wife of her own
was suspicious of the actual
existence of said good wife

found her purpose relatively early
tried to outrun it
smoke it out

74

drown it
always found her though

liked being alone
was always scurrying off
away from parties
friends
events
husbands

held trauma
strength
joy
was rather hyper-independent
at times a complete energy vampire

sometimes took too much
sometimes gave too much
emotionally
and in narrative

if she hurt you
she hopes you can forgive her
if you hurt her
know she has forgiven you

except you – fuck you

climbed a lot of mountains (literal and figural)
ok only a moderate amount of mountains
most labelled easy

was so often lonely
sad
grateful
gleeful

struggled with self care
self love
self esteem
all the selves
struggled inside her
fought like family
at dinner
bickering
feeding
loving
indifferent
ignoring one another
descending into silence as they digested

learned life really got going when
she embraced the contradiction of it all

strove to honour
those who came before
make space
for those after
be a good ancestor
be a good kid

failed a lot
tried again
still

rose
(if you will)

journeyed far (literal and figural)

was constant
in her heart
if never her mind
if she loved you
she still loves you

except you – fuck you

her grandmothers were always with her
every day

she was absolutely terrified
all the time

did it anyway

bury me dirty

for my sister

there's a beautiful ritual
you have learned

when someone passes
they are washed
you wash them
in cedar-steeped water
life cleansed with medicine

I don't need that
bury me dirty

I won't mind
low maintenance to the last
put my ashes in recycled jars
give them to my children
let them take me to rivers
oceans
drop me bit by bit
I will care for nothing

been thinking a lot of death
like dickinson over here
with all these funerals in my head
or lack thereof
don't want one of those either
maybe a playlist
some good singing songs

let your Ceremony for me
be you alone in your car
with your favourite singing song
don't worry cars make you invisible in there
so you can really get into it

it's not that I want to go
don't think I will
I persist
piece by piece
with the cockiness of a strong genealogy
long life line
I will be
just another old tattooed Aunty
going on and on
giving less and less fucks
I want to make it all the way to none
spend a couple decades there
just living
smudging
smoking my pipe
see I get a lot of medicines
no need to waste more
when I'm gone
no need for anything
let my last favour to you be
one less thing to do

I have considered that
I just don't want you to see me naked
that could be all this is
but I don't care about being dirty

I'm going into the river
ocean
I will be nothing more than
sediment
sand
soon enough

Matriarchy/dreamtime

my mother
grandmother
all their sisters
openly talked about their dreams
how in their dreams they would see
the future

the final conversation my ninety-plus
grandmother had with her last-alive sister
so the story goes
was about their dreams
their dreams that told the future
as sure as schedules
what was going to happen
don't know what they talked about
only that they spoke lightly
a joke among intimates
a knowing among the knowledgeable

to know this story
is to know my matriarchs
my mom and her mothers before her
mennonite for generations
white ladies
from russia
germany before that
an easterly route
kicked out of countries one by one
before they got to come to canada
to settle on stolen land

mennonites are a sect of anabaptists
who have lived in relative isolation for centuries
the kicking around being out of religious persecution
back where white people only had each other
to kick around

my mother's family is downright secular
by comparison
amongst this uber-christian kind of people
whose basic general rules
by me (basically outsider)
are as follows:

no flashiness
no bragginess
no loudness (all these have a * *especially*
       women tacked on)
no worldliness (aforementioned)
no lifestyle but their lifestyle
no education (or at least no worldly education
       can ever be above the word of god)
no dancing
no promiscuity (obvs)
no drunkenness (except of course in closets.
       Lots of things happening in closets over there)

closed communities with many closed minds
keeping safe from another round of kicking
a chosen people
chosen as much for their divinity
as their commitment to follow the rules

so really
not the sort of place you'd think to get
dream teachings

I have learned a few dream teachings
from Anishinaabe Ininew and Michif folks
wherein there is an overall lesson about
listening to your dreams
your dreams contain things you need to know
things you forgot that you need to remember
they are your ancestors talking to you
the spirit world calling
they can help if you know
how to read them
should be shared considered discussed
            with Elders
when Knowledge Holders are asked for guidance
            —they dream
when people are given their names—those come
            from dreams
a dream can connect heal ease cure
that is the way as I understand it

I've never heard any official mennonite teaching
about dreams
the only teachings I remember are:
men eat first
dancing leads to sex
women dressing provocatively leads to sex
women are at fault when sex happens
sex is of course bad
all opinions are determined by the church

the devil causes worldliness—something to do with
     temptation
worldliness is of course very bad
funerals are times to repent repent repent—
     get in here quick they say
     heaven is an ever-closing door
     god forbid (literally) you don't make it
     and then die
     and go to hell
     (hell is of course is the worst worst)
     (though in description sounds pretty fun)

I don't imagine the folks who don't even like
Hallowe'en have much to say about
dream teachings
(but what do I know)

still my grandmother
dreamt the future
all of her life
and she told her sister about her dreams
one last time

I don't know what they specifically said
that's not a part of the story I know
doubtless an Aunty does
I hope one day they will tell me
I bet it's super important
or at least interesting
singular
significant

I know this because
I dream the future too
never anything big
no lottery numbers
or anything useful like that
it only ever comes in waves
waves over waves of possible outcomes
there are so many things
that never come to pass
only ever one path taken
the tangibles I remember are only
pieces
seemingly small things
I only know when they happen
when my whole body remembers
and I am certain I have to pay attention
because this is something I have dreamt
before:
my daughter's smile
helping my baby down the stairs
a long beach day
a mood that needs to be broken
safety

tiny but it's always been
the little things
that are most important

we know this because this is
what the grandmothers said

I like to think before they were mennos
if you reach back all those generations
through czarian russia
across germany
maybe even into the netherlands
where it all started
before the priests turned ministers
before the priests even came north
and stole all the pagan things
back then when my grandmothers
lived in bush amongst wolves
and were called something else entirely
they knew their dreams
shared lessons so strong they lasted
a dozen generations
made it all the way to those little old ladies
who never learned to dance
but still shared their dreams
in whispers
giggles
knowing

grandmother

you will grow old
your flesh will fall
like a map your skin
will draw deep lines

and mounds will peek
out of lovely brown freckles
cheeks will turn
the colour of a fish's belly
and be rough to the touch
like scales

what you think is your beauty
will sneak away from you
will go without a note
or goodbye
you will mourn this
you will rage against that
long lonely evening
when you realize what you think
is your beauty will never return

but your face will crater
and line with reflection
the grey will glow
the day will die
and you will rise
up into the brilliant night
be brighter
than you have ever hoped to be

you will
take your place amongst
the Elders
you will be
what you have always known
you should have always been

Peyahtik

then one day I realized
if I deny my voice
I deny my grandmothers
my many mothers
before my mother
as inadequate as I may be
I am all they have

I am afraid of everything
but them
their flawless spirits
long cleansed in the wind
these ghosts
tell good stories
in slow sugary voices
give them to me
explain those truths
I do not yet know
how to say out loud

it's shit or get off the pot time again
they say when I want to give up

their brown and browned faces fixed on me
their grins the wide prairie sky

go now
they shoo me along
be good

acknowledgements

Maarsii to everyone at Anansi: Kevin, Emma, Leslie, Alysia, Lucia, Semareh, all the many minds that it takes to make these things. Maarsii as well to Marilyn Biderman and the whole Transatlantic team. Big big maarsii to Tracy Fehr on all her work on that gorgeous cover.

These poems come from so many things over so many years and there are so many folks to thank. Nothing happens in a vacuum and no poem is ever written without a whole world. Maarsii to my home, community, family and all the many people who have given me opportunities to speak, share and live in story.

My kids. Only and all.

notes

A version of *grimoire*, titled *before i was this*, was featured in
Other Tongues: Mixed-Race Women Speak Out, edited by Adebe
DeRango-Adem and Andrea Thompson, Inanna 2010

if it were a river—ndn city, *Prairie Fire* 38.1, 2017

*Aaniin, Biindigen, Anishinaabemowin, Nimaamaa Aki,
Nookomis Giizis* in *Room* 41.2, 2018

behold the Matriarchs and *your body is a sovereign nation*
were inspired by the work of, written for and first read at a
March 8, 2023, event at the North End Women's Centre

Finally,

Biindigen—features riddle poems, inspired by the work of
Mary Dalton

carry memory—poems describe actual photos of my family,
Ernest Senior and Junior, Alma, Esther, Pierre Vermette

her story, notes—from a meeting with Prof. Susan Close, author
of *Framing Identity*, a long lunch we spent poring over my old
family photos

Peyahtik was a word I first found in the work of Gregory
Scofield and it's stayed with me ever since

Chi maarsii, all

katherena vermette (she/her/hers) is a Michif (Red River Métis) writer from Treaty 1 territory, the heart of the Métis Nation, Winnipeg, Manitoba, Canada.

Born in Winnipeg, her Michif roots on her paternal side run deep in St. Boniface, St. Norbert and beyond. Her maternal side is Mennonite from the Altona and Rosenfeld area (Treaty 1). In 2013, her first book, *North End Love Songs* (Muses' Company), won the Governor General's Literary Award for Poetry. Since then, her work has garnered awards and critical accolades across genres. Her novels *The Break* (House of Anansi), *The Strangers*, *The Circle*, and, most recently, *real ones* (Hamish Hamilton), have all been national best-sellers and won multiple literary awards, and her work for children and young adults includes the picture book *The Girl and the Wolf* (Theytus) and the graphic novel series A Girl Called Echo (Highwater). She holds a Master of Fine Arts from the University of British Columbia and an honorary Doctor of Letters from the University of Manitoba.

katherena lives with her family in a cranky old house within skipping distance of the temperamental Red River.